top dog knits

12 QuickKnit Fashions for Your BIG Best Friend

Jil Eaton

Photography by Nina Fuller

Breckling Press

Library of Congress Cataloging-in-Publication Data
Eaton, Jil,
 Top dog knits : 12 quickknit fashions for your big best friend / Jil Eaton.
    p. cm.
  ISBN 1-933308-16-8 (pbk.)
  1. Knitting--Patterns. 2. Dogs--Equipment and supplies. 3. Sweaters. I. Title.

TT825.E2863 2006
746.43'20432--dc22

Every effort has been made to be accurate and complete with all the information in this book. The publisher and the author cannot be responsible for differences in knitters' abilities, typographical errors, techniques, tools or conditions or any resulting damages or mistakes or losses.

Editorial direction by Anne Knudsen
Cover and interior design and production by Maria Mann
Series design by Bartko Design Inc.
Photography direction and styling by Jil Eaton
Cover and interior photographs by Nina Fuller
Pattern design by Jil Eaton
Learn-to-knit illustrations by Joni Coniglio
Drawings by Jil Eaton
Schematics by Jane Fay
Technical writing and editing by Carla Scott
Pattern proofing and editing by Janice Bye
Knit samples by Nita Young, Shirley LaBranch, Lucinda Heller, Pam Tessier, Janice Bye, Lynn McCarthy, Monte Nikkel, Eroica Hunter, Stephanie Doben, Barbara Elmore, Joan Cassidy, and Jil Eaton

This book was set in Syntax and Avenir
Printed in China

Published by Breckling Press, a division of Knudsen, Inc.
283 Michigan Street, Elmhurst, IL 60126, USA

Dedication

To Judith Shangold, my long time distributor, collaborator, colleague, brilliant business woman, and friend.

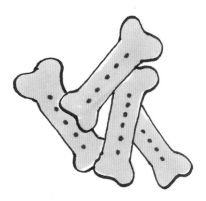

Contents

Woof, woof!

Rex . . . Rover . . . Butch . . . Moxie—the big guys are all Top Dogs in my book. Dogs are the most extraordinary creatures. Simple, strong, steadfast, fearless, loving, obedient, funny, curious and friendly, they are our best friends and companions, protectors and jesters. We are so lucky to share our world with them. And many, such as the elegant Greyhounds, the powerful German Short-Haired Pointers, the gorgeous Weimeraners, and the delightful Dalmations are actually very shorthaired, needing the warmth and protection of a felted jacket or hand-knit sweater on brisk morning walks. Greyhounds even wear neck-warmers on the coldest days, keeping their long lovely necks cozy and warm. Then there are those who just plain like to dress up . . . Poodles, in particular, love to sashay about decked out in their finery. So get your needles and get knitting—because, Fido, it's cold outside! And remember, when we are knitting, all is right with the world.

Jil Eaton

Jil Eaton
Portland, Maine

Gone to the Dogs!

The big idea for this collection of sweaters and jackets for large and mid-size breeds came from my photographer Nina Fuller whose brother's dogs are true Top Dogs. The term *Top Dog* refers to rescue animals who are trained to search and recover. They are hard-wired operators just waiting for the next command from their beloved masters. There are so many fabulous working dogs, from seeing-eye dogs to companions for the handicapped to police dogs, all admirable in their working roles. Now we love our charming house pets every bit as much, even if their hardest job is being on guard when we're not home! In this collection, our jackets and sweaters work with the larger breeds, maintaining their dignity while keeping them chic and warm. There is a classic cabled turtleneck sweater, several weatherproof felted jackets, and even pillbox chapeaux for sister poodles Jackie Onassis and Ivana Trump! The jackets are especially worth the extra effort of the felting process. I love felting, as it magically transforms knitted yarn into a wonderful thick, soft, weatherproof material. I have found these felted jackets to be just fabulous on my own top dog, Rexi-Martine, a Cock-a-poo. She has worn her jacket throughout the winter, in rain and snow and sleet and mud, and it still looks perfect. It is a show-stopper on the street as well!

As a knitter, I believe you should work with the highest quality yarns you can find; the hours spent working on an individual project warrant the best in materials, especially for your dogs, as they run and romp, stretching the fabric to its limits. Always look for the most beautiful colors and fibers. Natural fibers make the best sweaters, as they breathe and felt and wear like iron—perfect for dog sweaters or jackets. Color is especially variable, and dogs come in every shape, size and colorway—do adapt these projects and customize them for your own pet.

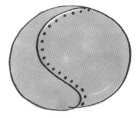

Knitting to Fit Fido!

Pooches come in all shapes and sizes. While all the designs in *Top Dog Knits* are intended for larger and midsize dogs, each breed has its own peculiarities. To make sure your finished garment fits comfortably, pay close attention to the following preparatory steps.

GETTING THE GAUGE

The single most important step when beginning any knitting project is to do a gauge swatch. The gauge swatch is a 4"/10 cm square, knit in the pattern called for and with the recommended

Knitting Kit

A clear zippered case, like those used for cosmetics, is best for the perfect knitting kit. Everything is visible and it's easy to fish out items you need. If you set yourself up with the following items, you have a portable studio, easily stashed in your knitting bag as you change venues or projects.

* Small, very sharp scissors, used only for yarn.

* Yarn needles: I like the Japanese Chibi needles with bent tips.

* Retractable measuring tape.

* Yarn T-pins and yarn safety pins for marking or holding dropped stitches.

* Stitch holders, both long and short. English Aeros are my favorites, but Japanese holders that are open at either end are also fabulous.

needle size. Getting the correct gauge, or number of stitches per inch, allows you to make a fabric that is even and smooth, with the correct drape and hand, resulting in the correct size. Any garment that is off the gauge one stitch per inch may end up five inches too big or small! Simply doing your gauge swatch will ensure a happy result, every time. It also can become part of your knitting history, and is perfect for testing washability and felting.

Using the needles suggested in the pattern, cast on the correct number of stitches to make a 4"/10 cm swatch, plus six more stitches. Knit three rows. Always knit three stitches at the beginning and end of every row, and work straight in the pattern stitches called for until the piece measures 4"/10 cm. Knit three more rows and bind off. Lay the swatch on a flat, smooth

* Stitch markers: split-rings are good as they can be easily moved and removed.
* Cable needles: I use straight US sizes 3, 6 and 10.
* Point protectors, both large and small, to keep your work on the needles.
* Needle/gauge ruler—essential.
* Crochet hooks: one small, one large.
* "Dentists' tool," with one hooked end and one smooth end—invaluable.
* Pen and small notebook, for notes, figuring and design notes.
* Small calculator, which you will use constantly.

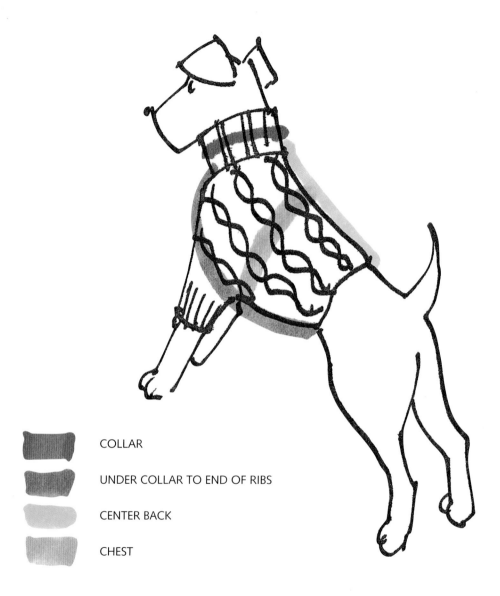

COLLAR

UNDER COLLAR TO END OF RIBS

CENTER BACK

CHEST

surface. Measure inside the garter stitch frame; you should have 4"/10 cm exactly. If your swatch is too big, or you have too few stitches per inch, change to a needle one size smaller. If your swatch is too small, or there are too many stitches per inch, change to the next larger needles. Getting into the habit of doing your gauge swatch will fine-tune your craftsmanship, making you a better knitter for life.

MEASURING YOUR TOP DOG

Our canine friends don't come in well-organized and standardized weights and sizes, so it might be necessary to adapt your pattern for your dog. Measure carefully:

Around the chest, just behind the front legs
Around the neck where the collar would sit
From collar to tail along the back ridge
From the under-collar to the end of the rib cage
Between the front legs

Review the schematic for your project, and make any necessary adjustments. The silhouettes are simple, and can be easily adjusted. Make sure you take the pattern into consideration, making changes that work with the math. Your local yarn shop may be a great resource for any necessary re-sizing as well. While doing the photography for this collection we found that the same sweater fit a Labrador, a German Short Haired Pointer and a Weimeraner!

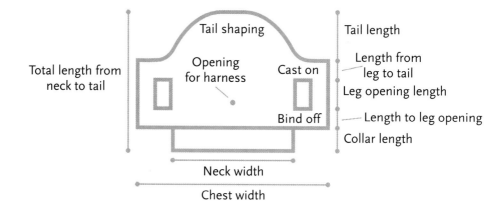

Tail shaping

Tail length

Total length from neck to tail

Opening for harness

Cast on

Length from leg to tail

Leg opening length

Bind off

Length to leg opening

Collar length

Neck width

Chest width

Shape One

Shape One is a pullover sweater worked from the neck to the tail, with a seam down the center of the under belly. The leg openings are bound-off, then each section is worked separately for a few inches. You next cast on new stitches above the bind-offs and work even to the tail shaping. Be sure to measure your dog carefully, including the width between the legs. If your dog has a lot of fur or has chubby legs, you may want a bigger opening. If your dog has very little fur, you may want to use fewer stitches in the bind-off.

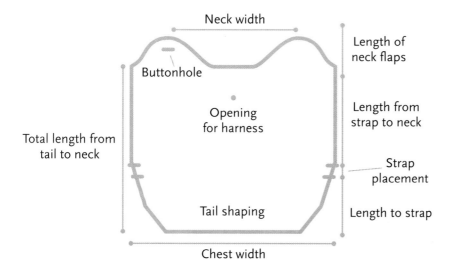

Neck width

Length of
neck flaps

Buttonhole

Opening
for harness

Length from
strap to neck

Total length from
tail to neck

Strap
placement

Tail shaping

Length to strap

Chest width

Shape Two

Shape Two is a jacket that buttons around the neck, with under-belly straps. It is worked and shaped from the tail to the neck. After the garment is finished, try it on your pup to determine where you should pick up stitches to knit the straps. We have included measurements for the strap placement, but it is easy to move them so your dog is more comfy.

RESCUE

*Here is Moxie, in
his service dog gear.
A true top dog!*

9

BLOCKING FINISHED PIECES

When you complete a project, cover each piece with two damp towels, one under and one over, pinning the pieces in place. Alternatively, you may pin the pieces to a blocking board, a wonderful invention that is widely available. Lightly steam at the appropriate setting for the yarn you are using, and dry your garment flat on a towel, mesh rack, or on the blocking board. Blocking usually improves the look of your garment, as long as it is gently done.

CARING FOR DOGGIE KNITS

You will want to launder your doggie sweaters, and your gauge swatches are absolutely perfect for testing the washability of a specific yarn, following the yarn label instructions. Most yarns are machine washable, if you put them on a very gentle cycle in tepid water. Place them in a small mesh bag, which holds their shape and gets them really clean. For wool, you should also use a no-rinse sweater soap such as Eucalan, which is available at fine yarn shops as well as on the Internet.

Learn to Knit

This learn-to-knit section takes you through the basic elements of knitting. Although there are many others, I have included only two types of cast-ons, the *knit-on cast-on* and the *cable cast-on*. Once you have mastered the knit-on method, you have actually learned the basic knit stitch. The cable cast-on is a variation on the same stitch and is used to form a sturdy, yet elastic edge.

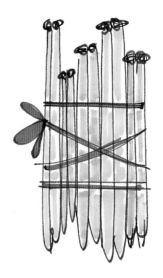

SLIP KNOT

1. Hold the yarn in your left hand, leaving a short length free. Wrap the yarn from the skein into a circle and bring the yarn from below and up through the center of the circle. Insert the needle under this strand as shown.

2. Pull on both the short and long ends to tighten the knot on the needle.

Step 1. Slip Knot

Step 2. Slip Knot

Step 1. Cast On

Step 2. Cast On

Step 3. Cast On

KNIT-ON CAST-ON

1. Hold the needle with the slip-knot in the left hand and the empty needle in the right hand. Insert the right needle from front to back under the left needle and through the stitch. With the yarn in the right hand, wrap the yarn around the right needle as shown.

2. With the tip of the right needle, pull the wrap through the stitch on the left needle and bring to the front.

3. Slip the new stitch off the right needle and onto the left needle. Repeat steps 1 to 3 for a simple knit-on cast-on.

Step 1. Cable Cast On

CABLE CAST-ON

1. Work Steps 1 and 2 of the knit-on cast-on above. Insert the right needle between the first two stitches on the left needle and wrap the yarn around the needle as shown.

2. With the tip of the right needle, pull the wrap through to the front.

3. Slip the new stitch off the right needle and onto the left needle. Repeat steps 1 to 3 for a cable cast-on.

Step 1. Basic Knit Stitch   Step 2. Basic Knit Stitch

BASIC KNIT STITCH

1. Hold the needle with the cast-on stitches in the left hand and hold the empty needle in the right hand. Insert the right needle from front to back into the first stitch on the left needle and wrap the yarn just as in the first step of the cast-on.

2. With the tip of the right needle, pull the wrap through the stitch on the left needle and onto the right needle. Drop the stitch from the left needle. A new stitch is made on the right needle. Repeat steps 1 and 2 until all the stitches from the left needle are on the right needle. Turn the work and hold the needle with the new stitches in the left hand and continue knitting back and forth.

BASIC PURL STITCH

The purl stitch is the opposite of the knit stitch. Instead of pulling the wrapped yarn towards you, you will push it through the back of the stitch. Because it is harder to see what you are doing, the purl stitch is a bit harder to learn than the knit stitch.

STEP 1. Basic Purl Stitch

1. Hold the needle with the cast-on stitches in the left hand and the empty needle in the right hand. Insert the right needle from back to front, into the first stitch on the left needle, and wrap the yarn counter-clockwise around the needle as shown.

2. With the tip of the right needle, pull the wrap through the stitch on the left needle and onto the right needle, as in the knit stitch. Drop the stitch from the left needle. A new stitch is made on the right needle. Continue in this way across the row.

STOCKINETTE STITCH

On straight needles, knit on the right side, purl on the wrong side. On a circular needle, knit every row.

GARTER STITCH

When knitting with straight needles, knit every row. On a circular needle, knit one row, purl one row.

DECREASE OR KNIT TWO TOGETHER (K2TOG)

Hold the needle with the knitted fabric in the left hand and hold the empty needle in the right hand. Insert the right needle from front to back through the first two stitches on the left needle. Wrap the yarn and pull through the two stitches as if knitting. Drop the two stitches from the left needle. One new stitch is made from two stitches; therefore one stitch is decreased.

Knit Two Together

INCREASE

Knit in the front of the stitch, and, without removing the stitch from the left hand needle, knit in the back of the same stitch, then drop the stitches from the left needle. This makes two stitches in one stitch.

BIND OFF

Hold the needle with the knitting in the left hand and hold the empty needle in the right hand. Knit the first two stitches. *With the left needle in front of the right needle, insert the tip of the left needle into the second stitch on the right needle and pull it over the first stitch and off the right needle. One stitch has been bound off. Knit the next stitch, then repeat from the * until all the stitches are bound off.

Bind Off

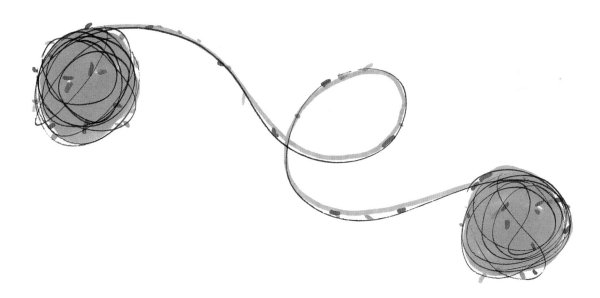

"This pullover sweater is perfect for me, considering my search and rescue profession. There is no question about my calling in this get-up! And all my pals are jealous, don't you know?"

Top Dog

If you've never tried intarsia, this is the project to begin with, as there is relatively little to do and the resulting effect is bold and charming. If you are really uncomfortable with intarsia, where you work the contrasting color on a separate bobbin, you could also do the entire sweater in one color and duplicate stitch the cross when you're done. Either way, the look is stunning.

●●● **Intermediate Beginner**

Finished chest: 22 (26, 30)"/56 (66, 76) cm
Length, neck to tail: 18 (20, 23)"/45.5 (50.5, 58.5) cm

MATERIALS

Worsted weight yarn: 330 (430, 570) yards/300 (390, 515) meters of MC; 110 (145, 190) yards/100 (130, 170) meters of CC
Straight needles: sizes 6 and 8 US (8 and 6 UK, 4 and 5 mm)
16"/40 cm circular needle: size 6 US (8 UK; 4 mm)
Double pointed needles (dpns), set of four: size 6 US (8 UK; 4 mm)
Stitch holders and markers

GAUGE

18 sts and 24 rows = 4"/10 cm over st and using larger needles

✓ *Always check gauge to save time and ensure correct yardage. Adjust needle size as necessary (see page 4).*

Dog Tag

NAME: Moxie, age 2

BREED: German Short Haired Pointer

SPECIALTY: Search and rescue, trailing, and cadaver recovery on land and under water

STYLE: "Clean, crisp color and a loose, comfortable fit"

Moxie exudes strength, agility, and sure-footedness. He proudly sports his Top Dog jacket, knit from Brown Sheep Lamb's Pride #M81 Red (MC) and #M11 White (CC)

*Measuring your dog can
be tricky—four hands are
definitely better than two.
Enlist a pal, as correct
measurements mean
a perfect fit.*

BODY

1. With smaller needles and MC, cast on 69 (81, 95) sts for the neck and work in k1, p1 rib for 3"/7.5 cm. Increase 30 (36, 36) sts evenly across the last (WS) row—99 (117, 131) sts.

2. Change to larger needles. Work in St st until the piece measures 6 (7, 8)"/15 (17.5, 20) cm from the beginning.

SPLIT FOR LEG OPENING

3. Next row (RS): Work 8 (10, 12) sts, then place the remaining sts on a holder. Continue on these 8 (10, 12) sts only for 4"/10 cm, ending with a RS row. Place sts on a second holder. Cut the yarn.

4. Rejoin the yarn and bind off the next 9 sts from the first holder for the leg opening. Work the next 65 (79, 89) sts only for 3"/7.5 cm, ending with a RS row.

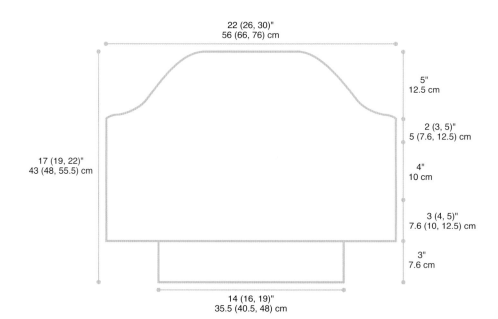

22 (26, 30)"
56 (66, 76) cm

5"
12.5 cm

2 (3, 5)"
5 (7.6, 12.5) cm

17 (19, 22)"
43 (48, 55.5) cm

4"
10 cm

3 (4, 5)"
7.6 (10, 12.5) cm

3"
7.6 cm

14 (16, 19)"
35.5 (40.5, 48) cm

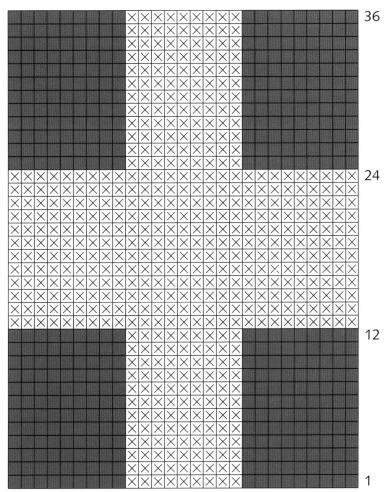

36

24

12

1

27 stitches

Color Key

■ Red (MC)

⊠ White (CC)

BEGIN CHART PATTERN

5. Next row (RS): Work 0 (5, 8) sts in MC, work 27 sts of the chart, work 11 (15, 19) sts in MC, work 27 sts of the chart, work 0 (5, 8) sts in MC. Continue in this way until this section measures 4"/10 cm. Place the sts on a third holder. Cut the yarn.

6. Rejoin the MC yarn and bind off the next 9 sts from the first holder for the leg opening. Work the remaining 8 (10, 12) sts for 4"/10 cm, ending with a RS row.

7. Next row (WS): Work the 8 (10, 12) sts on the needle. Cast on 9 sts, work 65 (79, 89) sts from the third holder (continuing in the chart pattern). Cast on 9 sts, then work the remaining 8 (10, 12) sts from the second holder. Continue on all 99 (117, 131) sts until the piece measures 12 (14, 17)"/ 30 (35.5, 43) cm or the desired length from the beginning.

Note: *After all chart rows have been worked, continue with MC only to the end of the piece.*

TAIL SHAPING

8. Bind off 4 (5, 6) sts at the beginning of each of the next 6 rows. Decrease 1 st each side every other row, 9 times. Bind off 5 sts at the beginning of each of the next 4 rows, then 4 (5, 6) sts at the beginning of the next 2 rows. Bind off the remaining 29 (39, 45) sts.

FINISHING

9. Block the pieces. Sew the center seam from the neck to the beginning of the tail shaping.

TAIL BORDER

10. With RS facing, a circular needle and MC, pick up and k 56 (66, 78) sts evenly around the tail shaping. Work in k1, p1 rib for 1"/2.5 cm. Bind off in rib.

LEG BORDERS

11. With RS facing, dpns and MC, pick up and k 58 sts evenly around each leg opening. Join and work in k1, p1 rib for 1"/2.5 cm. Bind off in rib. Block lightly.

"I've got many jackets,
but I've never had a
felted one before, and
I'll never go back to
anything else! You can't
believe how wind-proof
and even rain-proof it is
—I just wish I had an
umbrella, too . . . "

Bellissima

Bobbles are commonly knit and sewn on, but I prefer this simple and quick way instead. You take a long piece of the color for the bobble, thread it on a yarn tapestry sewing needle, and embroider through the felted fabric over and over, almost like a French knot. This trick is a great technique for scarves, as the bobbles are shown on both sides, making the piece reversible.

● **Beginner QuickKnit**

Finished chest (after felting): 13 (16, 22, 28)"/33 (41, 56, 71) cm
Length, neck to tail (after felting): 11 (13, 17, 22"/28 (33, 43.5, 56) cm

MATERIALS

Worsted weight yarn: 105 (150, 250, 420) yards / 95 (135, 225, 380) meters in MC; small amount in CC for bobbles
Straight needles: one pair size 10.5 US (3 UK, 6.5 mm)
Yarn sewing needle
Velcro for closing neck and straps: 2" x 6"

GAUGE

Before felting: 13 sts and 20 rows = 4"/10 cm over St st and using size 10.5 US (3 UK, 6.5 mm) needles
After felting: 14 sts and 23 rows = 4"/10 cm

✔ *Always check gauge to save time and ensure correct yardage. Adjust needle size as necessary (see page 4).*

Dog Tag

NAME: Sailor, age 5

BREED: Greyhound

INTERESTS: Hiking in the woods, playing with his best toy (a stuffed squeaky Santa), listening to classical music, eating spinach, and sleeping with his legs in the air!

STYLE: "Fred Astaire—cool and classy and very well-dressed."

This delightful concoction is knit in Manos del Uruguay #68 Citric (MC), with bobbles in #05 Aqua (CC). This is a perfect felting yarn and the hand-dyed color palette is delectable.

BODY

1. Beginning at the lower back edge and with MC, cast on 16 (24, 48, 64) sts. Knit 4 rows.

2. Row 1 (RS): k3, increase 1 st in next st, k to last 4 sts, increase 1 st in next st, then k3.

3. Row 2 and all WS rows: k3, increase 1 st in next st, p to last 4 sts, increase 1 st in next st, then k3.

4. Keeping the first and last 3 sts in garter st and the remaining sts in St st, continue increasing 1 st each side (inside of 3 garter sts as before), every row, 10 times more—40 (48, 72, 88) sts.

5. Work even, keeping 3 sts in garter st each side as before, until the piece measures 7-¼ (7-¼ , 12, 18)"/18.5 (18.5, 30.5, 45.5) cm or the desired length (accounting for shrinkage) from the beginning. End with a RS row.

Diagram reflects measurements *after* felting

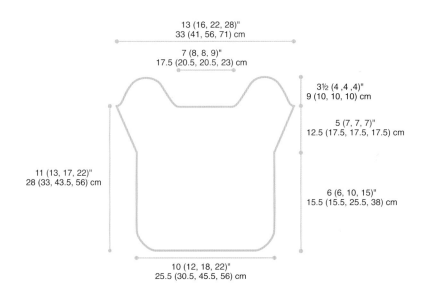

13 (16, 22, 28)"
33 (41, 56, 71) cm

7 (8, 8, 9)"
17.5 (20.5, 20.5, 23) cm

3½ (4 ,4 ,4)"
9 (10, 10, 10) cm

5 (7, 7, 7)"
12.5 (17.5, 17.5, 17.5) cm

11 (13, 17, 22)"
28 (33, 43.5, 56) cm

6 (6, 10, 15)"
15.5 (15.5, 25.5, 38) cm

10 (12, 18, 22)"
25.5 (30.5, 45.5, 56) cm

6. K 1 row. **Next row (RS):** k3, increase 1 st in the next st, k to the last 4 sts, increase 1 st in the next st, k3. Keeping 3 sts each side in garter st, continue to increase 1 st each side every fourth (fourth, fourth, second) row, 3 (3, 3, 4) times more, and every sixth (sixth, sixth, fourth) row 2 (4, 4, 7) times—52 (64, 88, 112) sts.

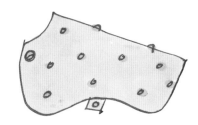

7. Work even until the piece measures 13-½ (16, 19-½, 25-½)"/ 34 (40.5, 49.4, 65) cm or the desired length (accounting for shrinkage) from the beginning.

8. K 1 row. **Next row (WS):** k3, p6 (10, 22, 32), k34 (38, 38, 42), p 6 (10, 22, 32), k3. Repeat the last 2 rows once more.

SHAPE NECK

9. Next row (RS): Keeping the first and last 3 sts in garter st and the remaining sts in St st, work 12 (16, 28, 38) sts. Join a second ball of yarn and bind off the center 28 (32, 32, 36) sts. Work to the end. Working both sides with separate balls, work 1 row even.

10. Row 1 (RS): k3, k2tog, k to last 5 sts on the first half, k2tog, k3; work the second half in the same way. **Row 2 (WS):** k3, p to the last 3 sts on the first half; work the second half in the same way. Repeating these 2 rows, continue to decrease 1 st each side (inside of the 3 garter sts) every sixth (fourth, second, second) row, 3 (5, 10, 5) times. *For the largest size only, repeat for 10 more rows.* Bind off the remaining 4 (4, 6, 6) sts on each side.

STRAPS

11. Place markers at the side edges of the body, approximately 6"/15.5 cm from the lower edge of the tail (or try on the dog to determine placement). With RS facing, smaller needles and MC, pick up and k 8 sts along one side edge above the marker. Work in St st for 4"/10 cm. Bind off. Work a second strap in the same way along the other side.

FELTING

12. Due to temperature fluctuations, felting time will vary. Check often for sizing. Set the washing machine on hot wash/cold rinse for a small load. Place the garment in the water with 1 tsp of liquid dishwashing detergent. Run through the longest cycle. Check the size, then run through again if necessary. Remove the garment, lay it flat, and let it dry.

BOBBLES

13. With CC, cast on 2 sts. **Row 1:** k3, increase 1 st—3 sts. **Row 2:** p3. **Row 3:** k2tog, k1. **Row 4:** p2tog. Cut the yarn, leaving a long tail and pull it through the loop. With a yarn sewing needle, sew the bobbles at random intervals around the sweater (see photo).

FINISHING

14. Sew Velcro to the center of the neck flaps and side straps.

Tips 'n Tails

Buy the very best yarns you can find, as fine yarns will result in a sweater that will keep your pup warm for years.

"Nothing like seeing the leash appear to get
a guy going . . . and what a leash this one is!
I might have chosen another color, but, hey,
fashion is fashion—who am I to quibble?
And the girls are giving me the eye. . ."

Who's Walking the Dog?

I-cord is a rather magical technique, and once you master it you will be using it all the time. With double pointed needles, cast on four stitches, knit, and slide to the right side of the needle. Without turning, bring the yarn in back across the stitches, and knit again. Repeat these steps, and suddenly there is a lovely tube of I-cord descending from your needles!

●● **Intermediate QuickKnit**
Finished length: 56"/132 cm

MATERIALS

Worsted weight wool: 105 yards/94.5 meters in colors A and B
Double pointed needles (dpns), set of two: size 8 US (6 UK, 5 mm)
Yarn sewing needle
Snap latch hardware: one (available at any hardware store)

GAUGE

5 rows = 1"/2.5 cm over I-cord

✔ *Always check gauge to save time and ensure correct yardage. Adjust needle size as necessary (see page 4).*

Dog Tag

NAME: Hunter, age 4

BREED: Weimeraner

INTERESTS: A recent Weimeraner National Specialties Best Veteran. Loves stuffed bears, has myriad girlfriends, and munches only organic cookie bones.

STYLE: "Cool and collected— real men wear pink."

This playful leash is made in Berroco Ultra Alpaca #6232 Light Pink and #6233 Rose

I-CORD

1. With 2 dpns and color A, cast on 4 sts. Slide the stitches to the right end of the needle and, without turning, k 4 sts. Continue in this manner until you have 64"/162.5 cm.

2. Change to color B and continue to 128"/325 cm.

3. Pull one end of the I-cord through the snap latch clip, centering at color change. Twist. With a length of A, tack the twists in place invisibly as you go.

HANDLE

4. Fold back 7"/17.5 cm for the leash handle. With matching yarn, sew through the remaining 4 I-cord sts to tack in place and form the handle.

Tips 'n Tails

Natural fibers or other easily washed fibers are the best choice for your pup's knits, since they will certainly need regular cleaning. Throw them in the washer using a no-rinse cleaner and voilà! Good as new.

"Run run, hunt hunt, flush flush, point point—whew! What a great hunting jacket, which is especially groovy for running though the piney woods. The padded spine cushion is essential—who knew?"

Blaze

The felting process is easy and fun—magic, almost. And the resulting thick, wooly, warm fabric is perfect for dog jackets. Fleecy and durable, these jackets are long-lasting after years of winter wear, perfect for any cold climate. They're even rain-proof, for those soggy days of autumn or West Coast living.

● **Beginner QuickKnit**

Finished chest (after felting): 13 (16, 22, 28)"/33 (40.5, 56, 71) cm
Length, neck to tail (after felting): 11 (13, 17, 22)"/28 (33, 43.5, 56) cm

MATERIALS
Worsted weight yarn: 95 (135, 250, 400) yards/85 (120, 225, 360) meters
Straight needles: one pair size 10.5 US (3 UK, 6.5 mm)
Velcro for closing neck and straps: 2" x 6"

GAUGE
Before felting: 13 sts and 20 rows = 4"/10 cm over St st and using size 10.5 US (3 UK, 6.5 mm) needles.
After felting: 15 sts and 24 rows = 4"/10 cm

✓ *Always check gauge to save time and ensure correct yardage. Adjust needle size as necessary (see page 4).*

Dog Tag

NAME: Red, age 3

BREED: Redbone Coonhound

INTERESTS: Hunting, romping with his day-care pals, and playing with 9-month-old Mia.

STYLE: "Old-world country, strong and sleek, I'm full of elegant gusto."

Red's sleek coat is a comfy choice for a night curled up by the fire or a run through the rain. Knit from Brown Sheep Lamb's Pride Bulky (#M110 Orange) and then felted to stand up to the toughest elements, he's sure to stay warm and dry.

BODY

1. Beginning at the lower back edge, cast on 12 (20, 32, 56) sts. K 4 rows.

2. Row 1 (RS): k3, increase 1 st in the next st, k to the last 4 sts, increase 1 st in the next st, k3.

3. Row 2 and all WS rows: k3, increase 1 st in the next st, p to the last 4 sts, increase 1 st in the next st, k3. Keeping the first and last 3 sts in garter st and the remaining sts in St st, continue increasing 1 st each side (inside of 3 garter sts as before), every row, 10 times--36

Diagram reflects
measurements
after felting

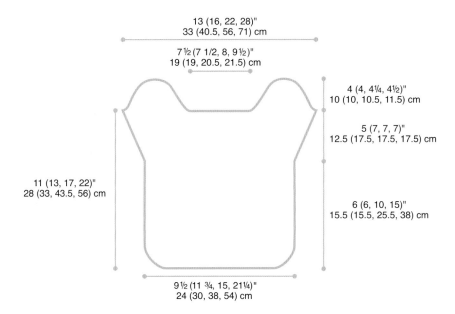

13 (16, 22, 28)"
33 (40.5, 56, 71) cm

7½ (7 1/2, 8, 9½)"
19 (19, 20.5, 21.5) cm

4 (4, 4¼, 4½)"
10 (10, 10.5, 11.5) cm

5 (7, 7, 7)"
12.5 (17.5, 17.5, 17.5) cm

11 (13, 17, 22)"
28 (33, 43.5, 56) cm

6 (6, 10, 15)"
15.5 (15.5, 25.5, 38) cm

9½ (11 ¾, 15, 21¼)"
24 (30, 38, 54) cm

(44, 56, 80) sts. Work even, keeping 3 sts in garter st each side and the remaining sts in St st as before, until the piece measures 7-¼ (7-¼, 12, 18)"/18.5 (18.5, 30.5, 45.5) cm from the beginning. End with a WS row.

4. **Next row (RS):** k3, increase 1 st in the next st, k to the last 4 sts, increase 1 st in the next st, k3. Keeping 3 sts each side in garter st, continue to increase 1 st each side every fourth row 5 (7, 5, 6) times, then every 0 (0, second, second) row 0 (0, 7, 5) times—48 (60, 82, 104) sts. Work even until the piece measures 13 (15-½, 20, 26)"/33 (39.5, 50.5, 66) cm or the desired length (accounting for shrinkage) from the beginning. End with a WS row.

5. K 1 row. **Next row (WS):** k3, p4 (10, 20, 28), k34 (34, 36, 42), p4 (10, 20, 28), k3. Repeat the last 2 rows once more.

SHAPE NECK

6. **Next row (RS):** keeping the first and last 3 sts in garter st and the remaining sts in St st, work 10 (16, 26, 34) sts. Join a second ball of yarn and bind off the center 28 (28, 30, 36) sts. Work to the end. Working both sides with separate balls, work 1 row even.

7. **Row 1 (RS):** k3, k2tog, k to the last 5 sts of the first half, k2tog, k3; on the second half, k3, k2tog, k to the last 5 sts, k2tog, k3.

8. **Row 2 (WS):** k3, p to the last 3 sts on the first half, k3; work the second half in the same way.

9. Continue to decrease 1 st each side, inside the 3 garter sts, every tenth (fourth, fourth, second) row, 2 (5, 2, 12) times, and every 0 (0, second, 0) row 0 (0, 7, 0) times.

10. Bind off the remaining 4 (4, 6, 8) sts each side.

STRAPS

11. Place markers at the side edges of the body approximately 6"/15.5 cm from the lower edge of the tail (or try on your dog to determine placement). With RS facing and smaller needles, pick up and k 8 sts along one side edge above the marker. Work in St st for 4"/10 cm. Bind off. Work a second strap in the same way along the other side.

FELTING

12. Due to temperature fluctuations, felting time will vary. Check often for sizing. Set the washing machine on hot wash/cold rinse for a small load. Place the garment in the water with 1 tsp of liquid dishwashing detergent. Run through the longest cycle. Check the size, then run through again if necessary. Remove the garment, lay it flat, and let it dry.

EPAULETTE

13. Fold the felted jacket in half, and with RS facing, sew a seam along the back , 2-½" (6.5 cm) from the back ridge. Open the jacket, lay flat, and fold the epaulette flat, evenly distributing the fabric on both sides. Using a blind stitch, sew the epaulette flat along sides and at the ends.

FINISHING

14. Sew Velcro to the center of the neck flaps and the side straps.

Tips 'n Tails

When knitting for your dog, make sure to do your gauge swatch. Getting the correct gauge makes the difference between a loose or tight garment and the perfect fit.

"When the cell phone rings, my ears are all atwitch and I'm ready to roll. But when I'm back at home and in my civies, this turtle neck is my favorite. Quite good-looking, don't you think?".

Cable Classique

You can make the turtle neck on this sweater as long or short as you like, depending on your dog or desire. This fold over classic is a great alternative to fleece jackets, and makes quite an elite fashion statement. The cables and seed stitch are easy to knit once you get the pattern established, and this will be a sweater your pooch will enjoy for many years. Clarke Gable would have loved this one!

●●●● **Advanced Beginner**
Finished chest: 14 (18, 23, 27)"/35.5 (45.5, 58.5, 68.5) cm
Length, turtleneck (unfolded) to tail: 24 (27, 30, 33)"/61 (68.5, 76, 84) cm

MATERIALS

Worsted weight yarn: 310 (450, 635, 820) yards/280 (405, 570, 740) m
Straight needles: one pair each, sizes 6 and 8 US (8 and 6 UK, 4 and 5 mm)
Double pointed needles (dpns), set of four: 6 US (8 UK; 4 mm)
Crochet hook: size G/6 (4mm)
Cable needle (cn)
Stitch holders and markers

GAUGE

22 sts = 3-½"/9 cm and 28 rows = 4"/10 cm over cable and seed st pattern using size 8 US (6 UK, 5 mm) needles

✔ *Always check gauge to save time and ensure correct yardage. Adjust needle size as necessary (see page 4).*

Dog Tag

NAME: Moxie, age 2

BREED: German Short Haired Pointer

INTERESTS: Training to be a professional search and rescue service dog, learning all the necessary skills with agility and intelligence. Moxie's older brother is the top rated Top Dog in Maine.

STYLE: "Bold and male, with a touch of Ralph Lauren."

When he's not in school, Moxie is all business in his debonair cabled sweater. Perfect for Brown Sheep Lamb's Pride Worsted yarn, this sample was knit with #M10 (crème).

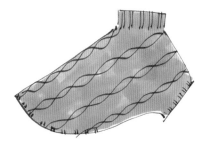

BODY

1. With smaller needles, cast on 92 sts for the neck and work in k2, p2 rib for 7 (8, 8, 9)"/17.5 (20.5, 20.5, 23) cm, increasing 1 (23, 56, 78) sts evenly across the last row--93 (115, 148, 170) sts. Change to larger needles and work in cable and seed st pattern until the piece measures 15 (16, 17, 18)"/38 (40.5, 43, 45.5) cm from the beginning.

SPLIT FOR LEG OPENING

2. Next row (RS): work 11 sts, then place the remaining sts on a holder. Continue on these 11 sts only for 4"/10 cm, ending with a RS row. Place sts on a second holder. Cut the yarn.

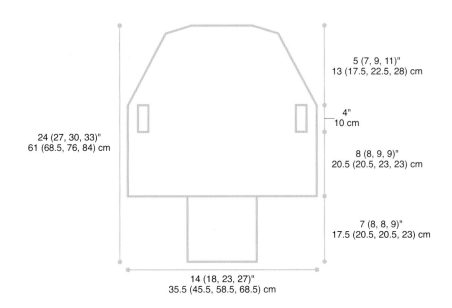

5 (7, 9, 11)"
13 (17.5, 22.5, 28) cm

4"
10 cm

24 (27, 30, 33)"
61 (68.5, 76, 84) cm

8 (8, 9, 9)"
20.5 (20.5, 23, 23) cm

7 (8, 8, 9)"
17.5 (20.5, 20.5, 23) cm

14 (18, 23, 27)"
35.5 (45.5, 58.5, 68.5) cm

Cable and Seed Stitch Pattern

(Multiple of 11 sts plus 5)

★ **Row 1 (RS):** [k1, p1] twice, k1, * k6, [k1, p1] twice, k1; repeat from * to end

★ **Rows 2, 4, 6 and 8:** k1, * [p1, k1] twice, p6; repeat from *; k1, [p1, k1] twice

★ **Row 3:** [k1, p1] twice, k1, *sl 3 sts to cn and hold to back, k3, k3 from cn, [k1, p1] twice, k1; repeat from * to end

★ **Rows 5 and 7:** Repeat row 1

Repeat rows 1 to 8 for cable and seed st pattern

3. Rejoin the yarn and and bind off the next 11 sts from the first holder for the leg opening. Work the next 49 (71, 104, 126) sts only for 4"/10 cm, ending with a RS row. Place sts on a third holder. Cut the yarn.

4. Rejoin the yarn and bind off the next 11 sts from the first holder for the leg opening. Work the remaining 11 sts for 4"/10 cm, ending with a RS row.

5. **Next row (WS):** work 11 sts on the needle, then cast on 11 sts. Work 49 (71, 104, 126) sts from the third holder. Cast on 11 sts and work the remaining 11 sts from the second holder.

Tips 'n Tails

Canine color choices are infinitely flexible. I prefer colors that are in contrast to the pup's fur, for a stand-out look.

TAIL SHAPING

6. Decrease 1 st each side every other row 15 (22, 33, 35) times—63 (71, 82, 100) sts. Place markers each side of on each side of the last row. Bind off 5 (6, 8, 8) sts at the beginning of the next 2 (4, 4, 4) rows, then 4 (0, 0, 7) sts at the beginning of the next 2 (0, 0, 2) rows. Bind off the remaining 45 (47, 50, 54) sts.

FINISHING

7. Block the piece.

LEG BORDERS

8. With RS facing and dpns, pick up and k 44 sts evenly around each leg opening. Work in k1, p1 rib for five rounds. Bind off in rib.

9. Sew the center seam from the beginning of the turtleneck to the markers, or to the desired length.

10. With RS facing and a crochet hook, work 1 row of single crochet evenly around the tail shaping, between the markers. Block lightly.

"Good golly Miss Molly, what a great looking coat! Every dog in the neighborhood will want one, I can tell the way they eye me now. And my brother Greaty is getting a matching outfit for Christmas— don't tell!"

La Parisian

I have discovered with my own pooch that felted jackets are absolutely fabulous. Try this one, either with the French Rosette trim as shown, with soutache, or with your own creative decoration or even monogram.

● **Beginner QuickKnit**

Finished chest (after felting and including straps): 22" (26)"/56 (66) cm
Length, neck to tail (after felting): 21 (22)"/53 (56) cm
Hat circumference (after felting): approx 17.5 (19)"/44.5 (48) cm

MATERIALS
Worsted weight yarn which will obtain gauge given below:
Sweater: 105 (150, 250, 420) yards/95 (135, 225, 380) meters
Hat: 90 (100) yards/ 80/90 meters
Straight needles, one pair (for sweater): **size 10 US (3 UK, 6.5 mm)**
Double-pointed needles (dpns), set of five: **size 10 US (3 UK, 6.5 mm)**
16" circular needle (for hat): **size 10 US (3 UK, 6.5 mm)**
Crochet hook for soutache: **size H/7 (5mm) (optional)**
¼" elastic for pillbox hat: 2"
Velcro for closing neck and straps: 2" x 6"

GAUGE
Before felting: 13 sts and 20 rows = 4"/10 cm over St st, and using size 10.5 US (3 UK, 6.5 mm) needles
After felting: 16 sts and 24 rows = 4"/10 cm

✓ *Always check gauge to save time and ensure correct yardage. Adjust needle size as necessary (see page 4).*

Dog Tag

NAME: Jet, age 4

BREED: Standard Poodle

INTERESTS: Eating birthday cake, cavorting with his brother Greaty, a white Standard Poodle.

STYLE: "Off-beat and easy, a comfortable way of going through the world. I'm an Aquarius, can't you tell?"

Burrr! It's cold outside! Yet Jet is hot to trot in his felted jacket knit from Manos del Uruguay #04 (turquoise). He'll be warm and happy on a cool walk to the store for some of his favorite treats--quiche and caviar!

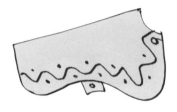

BODY

1. Beginning at the lower back edge, cast on 16 (24, 48, 64) sts. K 4 rows.

2. Row 1 (RS): k3, increase 1 st in next st, k to last 4 sts, increase 1 st in next st, k3.

3. Row 2 and all WS rows: k3, increase 1 st in next st, p to last 4 sts, increase 1 st in next st, k3.

4. Keeping the first and last 3 sts in garter st and the remaining sts in St st, continue, increase 1 st each side (inside of 3 garter sts as before), every row, 10 times more—40 (48, 72, 88) sts.

5. Work even, keeping 3 sts in garter st each side as before, until the piece measures 17-¼ (17-¼, 12, 18)"/18.5 (18.5, 30.5, 45.5) cm from the beginning. End with a WS row.

Diagram reflects measurements *after* felting

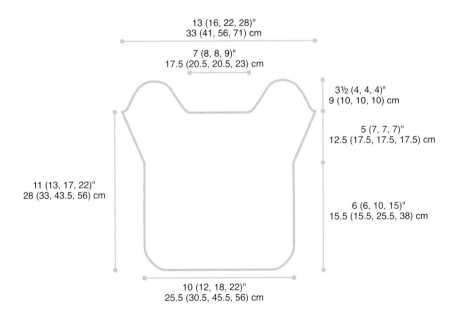

13 (16, 22, 28)"
33 (41, 56, 71) cm

7 (8, 8, 9)"
17.5 (20.5, 20.5, 23) cm

3½ (4, 4, 4)"
9 (10, 10, 10) cm

5 (7, 7, 7)"
12.5 (17.5, 17.5, 17.5) cm

11 (13, 17, 22)"
28 (33, 43.5, 56) cm

6 (6, 10, 15)"
15.5 (15.5, 25.5, 38) cm

10 (12, 18, 22)"
25.5 (30.5, 45.5, 56) cm

6. Next row (RS): k3, increase 1 st in next st, k to last 4 sts, increase 1 st in next st, k3. Keeping 3 sts each side in garter st, continue to increase 1 st each side every fourth (fourth, fourth, second) row 3 (3, 3, 4) times more, and every sixth (sixth, sixth, fourth) row 2 (4, 4, 7) times—52 (64, 88, 112) sts. Work even until the piece measures 13-½ (16, 19-½, 25-½)"/34 (40.5, 49.5, 65) cm or desired length (accounting for shrinkage) from the beginning. End with a WS row.

7. K 1 row. **Next row (WS):** k3, p6 (10, 22, 32) k34 (38, 38, 42), p6 (10, 22, 32), k3. Repeat the last 2 rows once more.

SHAPE NECK

8. Next row (RS): Keeping the first and the last 3 sts in garter st and the remaining sts in St st, work 12 (16, 28, 38) sts. Join a second ball of yarn and bind off the center 28 (32, 32, 36) sts. Work to the end. Working both sides with separate balls, work 1 row even.

9. Row 1 (RS): k3, k2tog, k to the last 5 sts on the first half, k2tog, k3; on the second half, k3, k2tog, k to the last 5 sts, k2tog, k3.

10. Row 2 (WS): k3, p to the last 3 sts on the first half, k3; work the second half in the same way. Continue to decrease 1 st each side (inside of 3 garter sts) every sixth (fourth, second, second) row, 3 (5, 10, 5) times. *For the largest size only, continue to decrease every row 10 times.* Bind off the remaining 4 (4, 6, 6) sts on each side.

STRAPS

11. Place markers at the side edges of the body, approximately 6"/15.5 cm from the lower edge of the tail (or try on the dog to determine placement). With RS facing and smaller needles, pick up and k 8 sts along one side edge above the marker. Work in St st for 4"/10 cm. Bind off. Work a second strap in same way along the other side.

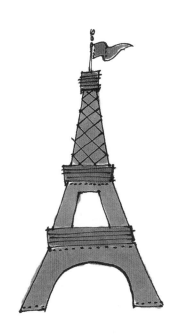

FELTING

12. Due to temperature fluctuations, felting time will vary. Check often for sizing. Set the washing machine on hot wash/cold rinse for a small load. Place the garment in the water with 1 tsp of liquid dishwashing detergent. Run through the longest cycle. Check the size, then run through again if necessary. Remove the garment, lay it flat, and let it dry.

FINISHING

13. Sew a 2" x 3" square of Velcro to each side of the jacket neck and on the straps.

Rosette Ribbon Flower (optional)

14. Cut three pieces of ribbon each 12"/30.5 cm long for one flower. Fold the ends to the center, allowing them to overlap until the length is about 5"/13 cm. Place them over each other to form a flower (see photo). Sew a button to the center to secure. Sew the rosette to the sweater as desired.

SOUTACHE TRIM (optional)

15. With CC and a crochet hook, work chain stitch for approximately double the length around the felted jacket. Leave the last st on a holder and sew around the jacket edge in a zig zag pattern. Work around until you reach your starting point, adjust the sts, pull the yarn through the last stitch, and sew in place. Make French knot bobbles around the zig zags.

PILLBOX HAT

16. Cast 4 sts onto one dpn. Increase 1 st in each st on the next row—8 sts. Divide the sts evenly over four dpns (2 sts on each needle). Join, being careful not to twist the sts on the needles and work in rounds of St st (k every round), increasing 1 st at the end of every needle every round (therefore 4 sts increased every round) until there are 64 (68) sts, or 16 (17) sts on each needle.

Note: To make the hat smaller or larger, work a multiple of four fewer or four more increases.

17. To turn the ridge, k 1 rnd, p 4 rnds. Continue to k every rnd for 4"/10 cm, or desired depth (Note that felting will shrink the depth about 1"/2.5 cm). Transfer sts to a circular needle.

I-CORD BORDER

18. With two dpns, cast on 4 sts. **Row 1 (RS):** k4. Do not turn the work. Slide the sts to the other end of the needle. **Row 2:** k3, pulling the first st tightly, and k the last st together with the first st from the circular needle through its back loop, with RS facing; slide the sts to the other end of the needle. Continue in this way until all sts on the circular needle are bound off. Bind off the last 3 sts and sew the ends of the I-cord together.

I-CORD TIES

19. With two dpns, cast on 4 sts and work the I-cord as before for approx 5-½"/14 cm. **Next row:** k into the front and back of the next 2 sts and work the I-cord on these 4 new sts for approximately 3"/7.5 cm. K in the front and back of the remaining 2 sts and work the I-cord on these 4 sts for approximately 3"/7.5 cm. Make a second tie in the same way. Attach them to the inside of the hat, under the I-cord border.

20. Cut lengths of the elastic to fit under the dog's chin, and sew inside the pillbox just above the I-cord border.

21. Embellish the hat with a rosette flower or soutache trim, as before.

Jackie Onassis and Ivana Trump show off their outfits, complete with soutache trim! Quite the Jackie Kennedy look, circa 1964. Just the thing for covering our trade-mark top-knots, they stay put just so."

"Oooh la la, cherie,
c'est magnifique! Sans
doubt, c'est ma jupe
tres perfect, et je suis
pleine de la chic main-
tenant. Quand nous
sommes dans la ville,
toutes m'adore . . . "

Fleur de Lis

This alpaca is wonderful to work with, and the ruffles are easily knit since the roving has a slight twist. The pocket, perfect for doggie bags or treats, is picked up and then knit up, then the sides are sewn in place. The little ruffle at the top adds panache—a real QuickKnit full of style.

●● **Beginner QuickKnit**

Finished chest: 22 (25, 28)"/55 (63.5, 71) cm
Length, neck ruffle to tail ruffle: 20.5 (22.5, 24.5)"/52 (57, 62) cm

MATERIALS

Worsted weight yarn: 470 (600, 720) yards/425 (540, 650) meters
Straight needles: size 8 US (6 UK, 5 mm)
32"/81 cm circular needle: size 8 US (6 UK, 5 mm)
Crochet hook for soutache: size H (5 mm)
Velcro for straps: 2" x 3"

GAUGE

15 sts and 22 rows = 4"/10 cm over St st and using size 8 US
(6 UK, 5 mm) needles

✔ *Always check gauge to save time and ensure correct yardage.
Adjust needle size as necessary (see page 4).*

Dog Tag

NAME: Daisy, age 5

BREED: Standard Poodle

INTERESTS: Off-leash runs, all car rides, chasing helpless creatures, and listening to her father play jazz piano, a true Daddy's Girl

STYLE: "Tres chic, always elegantly coiffed and buffed, perfect for the runway!"

This elegant sample is knit in Toasted Lavendar Alpaca from The Fibre Company

BODY

1. Cast on 144 sts for the neck and work in k4, p4 rib for 6 rows.

2. Next row (RS): * [k2tog] twice, [p2tog] twice; repeat from * to the end—72 sts. Continue in k2, p2 rib for 3"/8 cm more, increasing 11 (22, 33) sts evenly across the last row—83 (94, 105) sts. Work in St st until the piece measures 15 (17, 19)"/38 (43, 48) cm or the desired length from the beginning to the tail shaping.

TAIL SHAPING

3. Bind off 4 (4, 5) sts at the beginning of the next 6 rows. Decrease 1 st on each side every other row, 9 times. Bind off 3 sts at the beginning of the next 4 rows. Bind off the remaining 29 (40, 45) sts.

RUFFLE BORDER

4. With the RS facing and a circular needle, pick up and k 156 (176, 192) sts evenly around the outside edge of the tail shaping. P one row on the

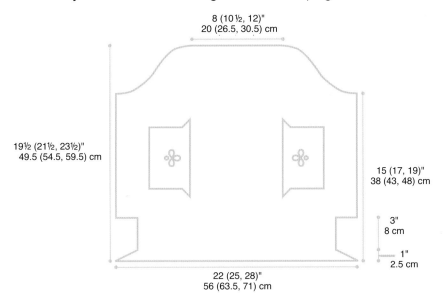

8 (10½, 12)"
20 (26.5, 30.5) cm

19½ (21½, 23½)"
49.5 (54.5, 59.5) cm

15 (17, 19)"
38 (43, 48) cm

3"
8 cm

1"
2.5 cm

22 (25, 28)"
56 (63.5, 71) cm

WS. Increase 1 st in each st on the next row to double the number of sts. Work in k4, p4 rib for 1"/2.5 cm. Bind off in rib.

POCKET WITH RUFFLE BORDER

5. Cast on 20 sts. Work in St st until the piece measures 5"/13.5 cm from the beginning. Purl 1 row on the WS.

RUFFLE BORDER

6. Increase 1 st in each st on the next row to double the number of sts—40 sts. Work in k4, p4 rib for 1"/2.5 cm. Bind off in rib.

FINISHING

7. Block the piece. Sew the turtleneck and ruffle seam.

SOUTACHE FLEUR DE LIS

8. Large top motif: with a crochet hook and CC, crochet 37. Fasten off. Following the photograph and the diagram, sew to the RS of the pocket. **Small bottom motif:** with a crochet hook and CC, crochet 2. Fasten off. Sew in place on the pocket below the large motif. Sew the pockets to the RS of the sweater, following the photograph and diagram.

STRAPS

9. Place markers at the side edges of the body approximately 6"/12 cm from the lower edge of the tail (or try on your dog to determine placement). With the RS facing, smaller needles and MC, pick up and k8 Sts under the ruffle along one side edge above the marker. Work in St st for 2-½"/6 cm or the desired length. Bind off.

10. Work a second strap in same way along the other side. Sew a 2" x 3" square of Velcro to the straps.

Chain Stitch with CC

*"In Maine, when it's cold,
it's cold! Neckwarmers keep
my long neck toasty, even in
the blustery winter chill. And
of course I love stripes—just
the thing for dapper me."*

Cozy Up

*Though we didn't know before we began this collection,
Greyhounds and other long-necked dogs actually need neck
protection on the coldest days. This pull-on ribbed and ruffled charmer is a cinch to knit, and would be adorable on any
dog, just for fun. Great for holiday presents, too.*

● ● ● ●   **Advanced Beginner**

Finished length: 8"/20 cm plus stand up 2.5"/6 cm collar
Finished neck circumference: approx 16"/40.5 cm

MATERIALS
Worsted weight yarn: 175 yards/160 meters in main color (MC):
150 yards/135 meters in contrast color (CC)
Straight needles: size 8 US (6 UK, 5 mm)

GAUGE
24 sts = 3.5"/9 cm and 28 rows = 4"/10 cm over rib pattern using
size 8 US (6 UK, 5 mm) needles

✔ *Always check gauge to save time and ensure correct yardage.
Adjust needle size as necessary (see page 4).*

Dog Tag

NAME: Pepper, age 4

BREED: Greyhound

INTERESTS: Gazing at the
ocean, and running through
the open fields at Hinckley
Park. Meeting and greeting
on the city streets, and
chasing squirrels and leaves.

STYLE: "First class all the way!"

*How would your favorite
friend like a neckwarmer like
this one, colorfully knit in
Berroco's Ultra Alpaca 6246
Green (MC) and 6239 Light
Blue (CC)*

NECK WARMER

1. With MC, cast on 110 sts and work in rib pattern and stripes as follows: *6 rows MC, 6 rows CC; repeat from * for the stripe pattern until the piece measures 8"/20.5 cm from the beginning.

COLLAR AND TIES

2. Work in garter st and continue in the stripe pattern, increasing 1 st each side (at 2 sts in from each edge) every other row, until the collar measures 5"/12.5 cm. Bind off.

FINISHING

3. Sew the ribbed section of the neck cozy for 7"/17.5 cm from the bottom. Fold the collar back inside the cozy and hem across, easing in any fullness to create a ruffled effect, at the same time leaving the ends free for knot. Tie a double knot.

Rib Pattern

(Multiple of 6 sts plus 2)

* **Row 1 (RS):** k1, *k4, p2: repeat from *, end p1

* **Row 2:** k the knit sts and p the purl sts

* Repeat rows 1 and 2 for rib pattern

"I'm born to hunt, but really I just love the dressing up! I admire the classic look, the demure touch of the black collar, and the plaid. Perfect for the country estate— or the city streets, for that matter."

Hunter

The plaid in this darling outfit is made with knit-in row stripes and crochet vertical rows, very easy, very chic. The collar is knit right on, adding stitches at the corners to allow for the fold and an easy drape. You can adjust the length if necessary, but make sure you take the stripes into account.

●●●● **Advanced QuickKnit**

Finished chest (including strap): 19 (22, 25, 28)"/48 (55.5, 63.5, 71) cm
Length, neck to tail: 18 (21, 25, 28)"/45.5 (53, 63.5, 71) cm

MATERIALS
Worsted weight yarn: 450 (600, 900, 1,000) yards/45 (55, 65, 80) meters in main color (MC); 50 (60, 70, 90) yards/45 (55, 65, 80) meters in contrast color (CC)
Knitting needles, one pair each: sizes 6 and 8 US (8 and 6 UK, 4 and 5 mm)
Crochet hook: size G/6 US (7 UK, 4.5 mm) for chain stitch
⅞" (2 cm) button
Velcro for straps: 2" x 2"

GAUGE
16 sts and 22 rows = 4"/10 cm over St st using larger needles

✔ *Always check gauge to save time and ensure correct yardage. Adjust needle size as necessary (see page 4).*

Dog Tag

NAME: Sadie, age 2

BREED: French Foxhound

INTERESTS: Co-piloting the Bug, Miles Davis, sleeping on her own futon, playing with her boyfriend, handsome Ben the Labrador.

STYLE: "Pretty and prim, lovely as an English rose."

Dress for the hunt in this classic jacket, knit up in Brown Sheep Lamb's Pride #81 Red (MC) and #05 Black (CC)

BODY

1. With larger needles and MC, cast on 33 (47, 57, 69) sts for the lower back edge, then k 4 rows. *(Note: work the first and last 3 sts in garter st and work the increase stitches in pattern stitch inside of these sts.)*

2. Next row (RS): k3, increase 1 st in the next st, k3 (1, 7, 13), [p1, k16] 1 (2, 2, 2) times, p1, k4 (1, 7, 13), increase 1 st in the next st, k3. **Next row:** k3, increase 1 st in the next st, work in pattern stitch to the last 4 sts, increase 1 st in the next st, k3. Repeat the last 2 rows until there are 61 (73, 85, 97) sts, ending with a WS row.

3. Begin stripe pattern and pattern stitch. **Next row (RS):** with CC, k4 (3, 8, 14), [p1, k16] 3 (4, 4, 4) times, p1, k5 (3, 8, 14). *(Note: This is row 1 of the stripe pattern and the purl stitches should line up.)*

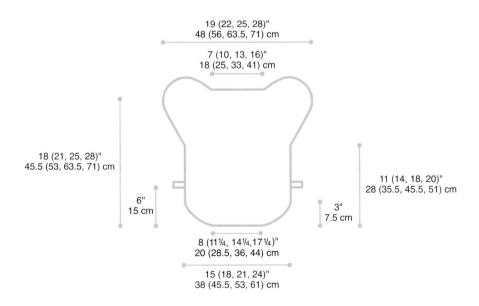

19 (22, 25, 28)"
48 (56, 63.5, 71) cm

7 (10, 13, 16)"
18 (25, 33, 41) cm

18 (21, 25, 28)"
45.5 (53, 63.5, 71) cm

11 (14, 18, 20)"
28 (35.5, 45.5, 51) cm

6"
15 cm

3"
7.5 cm

8 (11¼, 14¼, 17¼)"
20 (28.5, 36, 44) cm

15 (18, 21, 24)"
38 (45.5, 53, 61) cm

Pattern Stitch and Stripe Pattern

PATTERN STITCH

★ **Row 1 (RS):** k8, * p1, k16

Repeat from *, end p1, k8

★ **Row 2:** k3, k the knit sts and p the purl sts to the last 3 sts, k3

Repeat rows 1 and 2 for pattern stitch

STRIPE PATTERN

*1 row CC, 21 rows MC

Repeat from * (22 rows) for stripe pattern

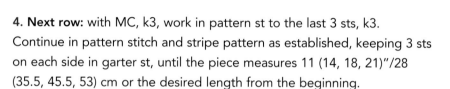

4. **Next row:** with MC, k3, work in pattern st to the last 3 sts, k3. Continue in pattern stitch and stripe pattern as established, keeping 3 sts on each side in garter st, until the piece measures 11 (14, 18, 21)"/28 (35.5, 45.5, 53) cm or the desired length from the beginning.

5. **Next row (RS):** k3, increase 1 st in the next st, k to the last 4 sts, increase 1 st in the next st, k3. Keeping 3 sts on each side in garter st, continue to inc 1 st each side (working increase sts into pattern stitch) every fourth row, 7 times more—77 (89, 101, 113) sts. Work even until the piece measures 17-½ (20-½, 24-½, 27-½)"/44.5 (52, 62, 69.5) cm or the desired length from the beginning, ending with a WS row. K one row.

6. **Next row (WS):** k3, p18, k35 (47, 59, 71), p18, k3. Repeat the last 2 rows once more.

SHAPE NECK

7. **Next row (RS):** keeping the first and last 3 sts in garter st and the remaining sts in St st, work 24 (30, 36, 42) sts. Join a second ball of yarn and bind off the center 29 sts. Work to the end. Working both sides with separate balls, work 1 row even.

Row 1 (RS): k3, k2tog, k to the last 5 sts on the first half, k2tog, k3; on the second half, k3, k2tog, k to the last 5 sts, k2tog, k3.

8. Row 2 (WS): k3, p2tog, p to the last 5 sts on the first half, p2tog, k3; work the second half in the same way. Repeat Rows 1 and 2 until there are 16 sts on each side. Continue decreasing as before and work a buttonhole in the center of the left flap by binding off 4 sts, then casting 4 sts onto the following row. Continue decreasing until there are 8 sts on each side. Bind off.

STRAPS

9. Place markers at the side edges of the body approximately 6"/12 cm from the lower edge of the tail (or try on your dog to determine placement). With RS facing, smaller needles, and MC, pick up and k 8 sts along one side edge above the marker. Work in St st for 4"/10 cm. Bind off. Work a second strap in the same way along the other side. Sew the Velcro to the strap ends.

FINISHING

10. Block the piece. With a crochet hook and CC, work chain st on top of each vertical line of p sts to form a plaid pattern. Sew a button on the right side of the neck, opposite the buttonhole.

COLLAR

11. With WS facing, larger needles, and CC, pick up and k 32 (45, 57, 69) sts evenly around the neck edge. **Next row (RS):** k2, increase 1 st in the next st, k to the last 3 sts, increase 1 st in the next st, k2. Continue in garter st, increasing 1 st each side every other row, until the collar measures 3-½"/9.5 cm or the desired length. Bind off.

*"When I'm training for my Service Dog work
I wear a special jacket so people know not to pat me
and to take me seriously. So when I'm off duty I can
wear anything I want, and this gorgeous sweater is the
tops! The colors suit my blond hair just perfectly!"*

Nordique

Everyone loves a traditional fair isle pattern, and this one is especially easy to knit, as you never have more than two colors going at once. The pullover style makes a very cozy sweater, perfect for those chilly winter days, and the gorgeous colors lend flair for the fashionable pooch. Working with colors may seem daunting, but here you are never working with more than two at a time, so it is easy going. The trick is to keep your tension looser than usual. Give it a try, you'll be delighted with the result!

● ● ● **Intermediate**

Finished chest: 13 (16, 22, 28)"/33 (40.5, 56, 71) cm
Length, neck to tail: 11-½ (13-½, 17-¼, 21-¼)"/29 (31, 43.5, 53.5) cm

MATERIALS
Worsted weight yarn: 100 (150, 200, 275) yards/90 (135, 180, 250) meters of A; 90 (100, 125, 135) yards/80 (90, 115, 120) meters of C; 50 yards/45 meters each of B, D, and E
Straight needles: sizes 8 and 9 US (6 and 5 UK, 5 and 5.5 mm)
Double-pointed needles (dpns): size 8 US (6 UK and 5 mm)
Stitch holders and markers

GAUGE
18 sts and 24 rows = 4"/10 cm over St st and Fair Isle chart pattern using larger needles

✔ *Always check gauge to save time and ensure correct yardage. Adjust needle size as necessary (see page 4).*

Dog Tag

NAME: Logan, age 18 months

BREED: Golden Retriever

SPECIALTY: A trained service dog for the handicapped

INTERESTS: A trained Service Dog for the Handicapped, she simply loves her work, swimming at Old Orchard Beach, and peanut butter.

STYLE: "Open and lovely, fresh and spirited."

Hand spun and hand dyed, this delicious wool is butter in your hands, and works up quickly in spite of the multi-colors. Logan's winter warmer is knit in Manos del Uruguay Calypso Q (A), Aqua 05 (B), Heliotrope 63 (C), Poppy 66 (D), and Citric 68 (E)

BODY

1. With smaller needles and A, cast on 32 (40, 56, 70) sts for the neck and work in k1, p1 rib for 2 (2-½, 3, 4)"/5 (6.5, 7.5, 10) cm, increasing 27 (33, 43, 57) sts evenly across the last (WS) row, to 59 (73, 99, 127) sts.

2. Change to larger needles. Work in St st and the chart pattern until the piece measures 3-½ (4-½, 5-½, 7)"/9 (11.5, 14, 17.5) cm from the beginning.

SPLIT FOR LEG OPENING

3. Next row (RS): work 7 (8, 8, 9) sts, place the remaining sts on a holder. Continue on these 7 (8, 8, 9) sts only for 2 (2-½, 3, 3)"/5 (6.5, 7.5, 7.5) cm, ending with a RS row. Place sts on a second holder. Cut the yarn.

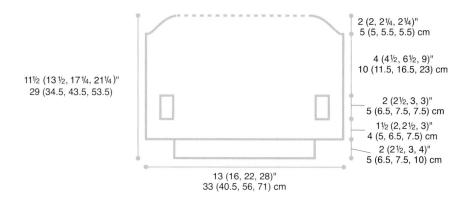

11½ (13 ½, 17 ¼, 21¼)"
29 (34.5, 43.5, 53.5)

2 (2, 2¼, 2¼)"
5 (5, 5.5, 5.5) cm

4 (4½, 6½, 9)"
10 (11.5, 16.5, 23) cm

2 (2½, 3, 3)"
5 (6.5, 7.5, 7.5) cm

1½ (2, 2½, 3)"
4 (5, 6.5, 7.5) cm

2 (2½, 3, 4)"
5 (6.5, 7.5, 10) cm

13 (16, 22, 28)"
33 (40.5, 56, 71) cm

4. Rejoin the yarn and bind off the next 6 (7, 8, 8) sts from the first holder for the leg opening, then work the next 33 (43, 67, 93) sts only for 2 (2-½, 3, 3)"/5 (6.5, 7.5, 7.5) cm . Place these sts on a third holder. Cut the yarn.

5. Rejoin the yarn and bind off the next 6 (7, 8, 8) sts from the first holder for the leg opening, then work the remaining 7 (8, 8, 9) sts for 2 (2-½, 3, 3)"/5 (6.5, 7.5, 7.5) cm, ending with a RS row.

6. Next row (WS): work the 7 (8, 8, 9) sts on the needle, cast on 6 (7, 8, 8) sts, then work 33 (43, 67, 93) sts from the third holder (continuing in the chart pattern). Cast on 6 (7, 8, 8) sts, then work the remaining 7 (8, 8, 9) sts from the second holder. Continue on all 59 (73, 99, 127) sts until the piece measures 9-½ (11-½, 15, 19)"/24 (31, 38, 48) cm or the desired length from the beginning.

TAIL SHAPING

7. Bind off 6 (8, 10, 12) sts at the beginning of the next 2 rows. Decrease 1 st on each side every other row, 5 (5, 6, 6) times. Place the remaining 37 (47, 67, 91) sts on a holder.

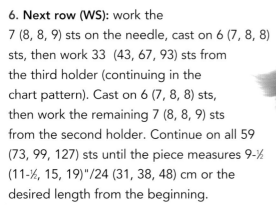

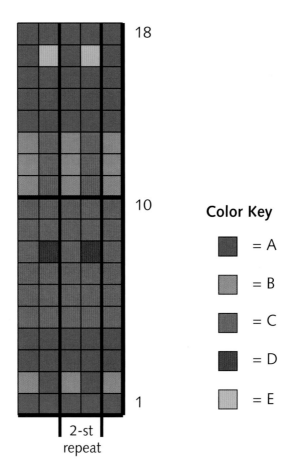

18

10

Color Key

= A

= B

= C

= D

= E

2-st
repeat

TAIL BORDER

8. With RS facing, a circular needle and A, pick up and k 16 (18, 22, 24) sts evenly along the side of the tail shaping. K 37 (47, 67, 91) sts from the holder. Pick up and k 16 (18, 22, 24) sts along the other side of the tail shaping—69 (83, 111, 139). Work in k1, p1 rib for 1" (2.5 cm). Bind off.

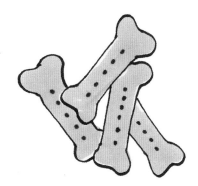

FINISHING

9. Block the pieces.

LEG RIBBING

10. With RS facing, dpns, and A, pick up and k 34 (38, 42, 42) sts evenly around each leg opening. Join and work in k1, p1 rib for 1"/2.5 cm. Bind off in rib.

11. Sew the center seam from the neck to the beginning of the tail shaping.

*"When I saw my reflection
in the mirror I was stunned—
who is that handsome chap?
This felted jacket is
amazing—let it snow,
let it snow, let it snow!"*

Sparky Stripes

The Velcro tabs sewn on the inside the chest pieces and the under-belly fasteners make donning this jacket a breeze, and the Velcro is sturdy and washable. If you prefer, unique buttons would work as well—simply use sharp shears to snip a button-hole opposite your button, and off you go.

- **Beginner QuickKnit**

Finished chest (after felting): 13 (16, 22, 28)"/33 (40.5, 56, 71) cm
Length, neck to tail (after felting): 11 (13, 17, 22)"/28 (33, 43.5, 56) cm

MATERIALS
Worsted weight yarn: 65 (90, 160, 260) yards/60 (80, 145, 235) meters in (A)
65 (90, 160, 260) yards/60 (80, 145, 235) meters in (B)
Straight needles, one pair: size 10.5 US (3 UK, 6.5 mm)
Velcro for closing neck and straps: 2" x 6"

GAUGE
Before felting: 13 sts and 20 rows = 4"/10 cm over St st and using size 10.5 US (3 UK, 6.5 mm) needles
After felting: 15 sts and 24 rows = 4"/10 cm
Black yarn felts more than white. Do a gauge swatch with 18 rows of each color.

✓ *Always check gauge to save time and ensure correct yardage. Adjust needle size as necessary (see page 4).*

Dog Tag

NAME: Pacco, age 5

BREED: Dalmation

INTERESTS: Running, jumping off the dock at camp, watching *Finding Nemo*, chasing rabbits and groundhogs, and eating strawberries.

STYLE: "Euro chic, handsome and elegant, and full of élan."

Pass the stripes, please! Pacco is oh so handsome in his black and white coat knit with Brown Sheep Lamb's Pride Bulk. The sample here uses #M11 White Frost (A) and #M15 Onyx (B).

Stripe Pattern

*18 rows A, 18 rows B; repeat from * (36 rows) for stripe pattern

BODY

1. Beginning at the lower back edge, with A, cast on 12 (20, 32, 56) sts. Knit six rows.

2. Row 1 (RS): k3, increase 1 st in the next st, k to the last 4 sts, increase 1 st in the next st, k3. **Row 2 and all WS rows:** k3, increase 1 st in the next st, p to the last 4 sts, increase 1 st in the next st, k3. Keeping the first and last 3 sts in garter st and the remaining sts in St st, continue increasing 1 st each side (inside of 3 garter sts as before), every row, 10 times more— 36 (44, 56, 80) sts. (18 rows of stripe pattern have been worked).

3. Work even, and continue in the stripe pattern (begin with B), keeping 3 sts in garter st on each side and the remaining sts in St st as before, until the piece measures 7-¼ (7-¼, 12, 18)"/18.5 (18.5, 30.5, 45.5) cm from the beginning, ending with a WS row.

4. Next row (RS): k3, increase 1 st in the next st, k to the last 4 sts, increase 1 st in the next st, k3. Keeping 3 sts on each side in garter st, continue to increase 1 st each side every fourth row 5 (7, 5, 6) times more, then every 0 (0, second, second) row 0 (0, 7, 5) times—48 (60, 82, 104)

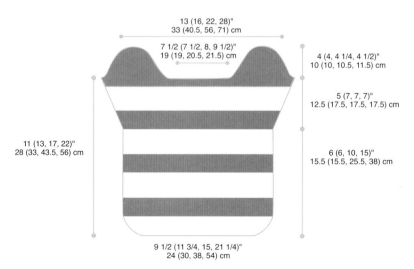

13 (16, 22, 28)"
33 (40.5, 56, 71) cm

7 1/2 (7 1/2, 8, 9 1/2)"
19 (19, 20.5, 21.5) cm

4 (4, 4 1/4, 4 1/2)"
10 (10, 10.5, 11.5) cm

5 (7, 7, 7)"
12.5 (17.5, 17.5, 17.5) cm

11 (13, 17, 22)"
28 (33, 43.5, 56) cm

6 (6, 10, 15)"
15.5 (15.5, 25.5, 38) cm

9 1/2 (11 3/4, 15, 21 1/4)"
24 (30, 38, 54) cm

sts. Work even until the piece measures 13 (15-½, 20, 26)"/33 (39.5, 50.5, 66) cm or the desired length (accounting for shrinkage) from the beginning, ending with a WS row. K one row. **Next row (WS):** k3, p4 (10, 20, 28), k 34 (34, 36, 42), p4 (10, 20, 28), k3. Repeat the last 2 rows once more.

SHAPE NECK

5. **Next row (RS):** Keeping first and last 3 sts in garter st and the remaining sts in St st, work 10 (16, 26, 34) sts. Join a second ball of yarn and bind off the center 28 (28, 30, 36) sts. Work to the end. Working both sides with separate balls, work 1 row even. **Row 1 (RS):** k3, k2tog, k to the last 5 sts on the first half, k2tog, k3; on the second half, k3, k2tog, k to the last 5 sts, k2tog, k3. **Row 2 (WS):** K3, p to the last 3 sts on the first half, k3; work the second half in the same way. Continue to decrease 1 st on each side, inside of 3 garter sts, every tenth (fourth, fourth, second) row 2 (5, 2, 12) times, and every 0 (0, second, 0) row 0 (0, 7, 0) times. Bind off the remaining 4 (4, 6, 8) sts on each side.

STRAPS

6. Place markers at the side edges 5"/13 cm from the lower edge of the tail (or try on for placement). With the RS facing, smaller needles and B, pick up and k 8 sts along one side edge above the marker. Work in St st for 4"/10 cm. Bind off. Work a second strap along the other side.

FELTING

7. With the machine on hot/cold rinse, with 1 tsp liquid detergent, run through the longest cycle. Felting time will vary, so check often for sizing. Dry flat.

FINISHING

8. Sew Velcro to the center of the neck flaps and to the side straps.

Lily: "I love my new monogrammed blankie. It's perfect for riding in the car, *and* it stays put very nicely, *thank* you. On the couch or in the library, it's my favorite perch! I just don't know how I ever slept without it . . ."

Pillow Talk

This project is a two-tiered delight. It is double-sided, with one side smooth and the other lattice stitched. Knit both sides and sew together, turn right sides out and sew I-cord in the gutter. Used flat it can be knit and monogrammed with your doggie's name or initials, or a favorite saying. Or it can be filled with a dog bed insert, and voila! A cozy, comfy dog bed!

* **Beginner**

Finished size: approximately 32" x 36.5"/81.5 cm x 92.5 cm

MATERIALS
Bulky weight yarn: 750 yards/675 meters each of color A and color B
Straight needles: size 10.5 US (3 UK, 6.5 mm)
Double pointed needles (dpns): size 10.5 US (3 UK, 6.5 mm)
Dog bed filler: 30" x 24" x 6" pillow form

GAUGE
14 sts and 19 rows = 4"/10 cm over Stockinette St using size 10.5 US (3 UK, 6.5 mm) needles

✓ *Always check gauge to save time and ensure correct yardage. Adjust needle size as necessary (see page 4).*

This perfect blanket is knit in Brown Sheep Lamb's Pride Bulky #M110 Orange (A) and #M-105 Pink (B)

Dog Tag

NAME: Lily (monogrammed blanket), age 1;
Izzy (dog bed), age 2

BREED: Lily—English Sheepdog;
Izzy—Portuguese Water Dog

INTERESTS: Lily likes barking, running on Willard Beach, herding and counting sheep, snacking on cookie bones, and sleeping in her owner's big bed. Izzy enjoys swimming, running marathons, playing with her pet bunnies, soft rock, and sleeping with Grace, her 8-year-old owner.

STYLE: "Bright and rambunctious, wild and wooly and full of charm." Lily

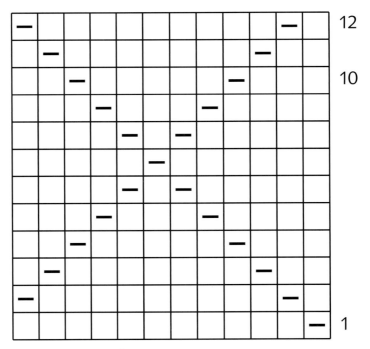

12 stitch repeat

Stitch Key

K on RS, p on WS

— P on RS, k on WS

FRONT

1. With color B, cast on 111 sts. Work in the chart pattern as follows: k1 (selvage st), work the 12-st repeat of the chart 9 times, then work first st of the chart once more, k1 (selvage st). Continue in pattern as established, keeping the first and last st of every row in garter st selvage, until the piece measures 36"/91.5 cm or the desired length. Bind off.

BACK

2. With color A, work the same as the front, but work in St st instead of in the chart pattern and keep selvage sts on each side.

I-CORD EDGING

3. With two dpns and A, cast on 3 sts.

4. * **Row 1 (RS):** k3, do not turn. Slide sts back to the beginning of the needle to work the next row from the RS, k3.

5. Repeat from * for the I-cord until it fits around the outside edge of pillow. Do not bind off.

6. With the RS of the front and back pieces facing, sew the two pieces together, leaving one short side open.

7. Turn inside out. For the blanket, blind stitch the remaining side. For the dog bed, stuff with a pillow form, and blind stitch the opening closed. Sew the I-cord trim around the outside edge of the pillow, in the gutter. Adjust the length of the I-cord if necessary, then bind off 3 sts and sew the ends together.

FINISHING

8. With color B, embroider the name of the dog using chain stitch on the Stockinette side of the blanket or dog bed.

Tips 'n Tails

Use your imagination! Knitting for your beloved pet can be a wonderful way to extend your own fashion sense.

Izzy: "Ah, bedtime. Grace let's me sleep in her room, all cozied up beside her bed. It's soft and cushy and warm. The minute I get home from my romp I dash to my wonderful new bed!"

Models and Merci

Whenever we are starting a new book we all forget the months of work, designing, technical pattern writing, knitting, propping, photography . . . and I am ever grateful for the boundless talents and energy from everyone involved. *Nina Fuller* takes all the gorgeous photography, and you can imagine how difficult shooting large canines can be. *Carla Scott* is the ever-brilliant technical genius who writes and edits the patterns. *Isabel Smiles* is my design guru. Thank you, thank you, thank you everyone!

Jil Eaton

Jil's life has always been full of dogs, many of them in the Top Dog category! Jeff, the enormous 80 pound white English Bull was first, then came Boy, a rescued Labrador stray, followed by Samantha, the 125-pound German Shepherd beauty, then Nina, the elegant Siberian Husky with translucent China blue eyes. Sam, an enormous lop-eared Shepherd came with her husband David, and then they adopted Zachary, a giant, soulful Great Dane/Pointer/Greyhound mix. Every one of them was a Top Dog, sans doubt! And now Rexi-Martine the blond Cock-a-poo rules the roost. She is quite the Top Dog even if she only weighs 18 pounds.

Educated in art at Skidmore College, Colby College and the Graduate School of Design at Harvard University, Jil Eaton's career as a painter and graphic designer finally succumbed to her early fashion instincts. She designs, publishes and distributes internationally an independent line of hand-knitting patterns under the Minnowknits™ label. Jil Eaton's designs have a comfortable, chic silhouette, melding the traditional with the new, adapting everything in easy-to-knit projects with great attention to detail, fresh styling and unusual colorways. Jil produces two pattern collections annually, designs for *Vouge Knitting International* and other publications, writes a feature column, "Ask Jil" in *Vogue Knitting's* latest magazine *Knit Simple*. She is now busy with her ninth book.

Nina Fuller

Nina Fuller is the one who so magically captures all these charming Top Dog models digitally. A nationally acclaimed location and studio photographer, Nina has degrees from Silvermine College of Art and George Washington University in Photography, Painting and Print-making. Location photography has been a creative focus for Nina, as well as photojournalism, as she trots from Great Britain to Australia on assignment for various publications, specializing in equine adventures. Her clients include LL Bean, Land's End, Horse & Hound, the Boston Globe, and Atlantic Records. She lives in Maine with her two children, two horses, a donkey, a mule, a pony, a pair of miniature goats, chickens, guinea hens, and her beloved Beso, a Giant Schnoodle.

Isabel Smiles

Isabel Smiles, design guru as well as location stylist, moved to Maine years ago after a successful run as a stylist and antiques & design shop owner in New York and Connecticut. She created the world-renowned Pomegranate Inn Bed & Breakfast, a stunning small hotel in Portland, Maine. She continues to do select freelance styling for the Meredith Corporation and Hearst Publications, as well as private design commissions. She is currently sans pooch, but spent many years with Nutmeg, a charming curly terrier.

Carla Scott

Carla Scott is my pattern writer, technical editor and a general knitting genius. Carla is without peer in her fabulous knowledge of knitting and garment structure, and since the beginning has been able to translate my sketches and swatches into written instructions and comprehensive charts. She is clear and calm amidst a mountain of math and engineering, and has an astute design eye. Carla is Executive Editor at *Vouge Knitting*, and clearly understands fashion as well as knitting; working with her is always delightful. She lives in New York City with her husband, daughter, and a pet fish.

The Knitters

My band of hand-knitters is the best on the planet! Knitting prototypes is tricky, and this Top Dog collection was quite a challenge, given odd shapes and sizing.

Big thanks to *Nita Young, Lucinda Heller, Shirley LaBranche, Pam Tessier, Eroica Hunter, Barbara Elmore, Janice Bye, Lynn McCarthy, Joan Cassidy, Stephanie Doben and Monte Nichol.*

The Models

Small dogs love the camera, but the big guys are anxious about the lights, have a hard time standing on the photographer's "seamless" background sheet, and are generally perplexed about the entire adventure. They intuit just where we want them to stand, and studiously avoid that in-focus, well-lit spot, to our collective annoyance. But they all did a great job in the end. Special thanks to all the wonderful owners who did their best dog-wrangling!

Top Dog: Moxie, a German Short-Haired Pointer
Blaze: Red, a Redbone Coonhound
Cable Classique: Hunter, a Weimeraner, and Enzo, a Labrador
Sparky: Pacco, a Dalmation
Bellissima: Hunter, a Weimeraner, and Sailor, a Greyhound
Fleur de Lis: Daisy, a Standard Poodle
Hunter: Bella, a French Foxhound
Nordique: Logan, a Golden Retriever
La Parisian: Jet, a Standard Poodle; Ivana Trump and Jackie Onassis, Standard Poodles
Cozy Up: Pepper, a Greyhound
Who's Walking the Dog? Hunter, a Weimeraner
Pillow Talk: Izzy, a Portuguese Waterdog, Lily, an English Sheepdog, and Logan, a Golden Retriever

Once again enormous thanks to my brilliant and esteemed publisher and editor, Anne Knudsen of Breckling Press. Thanks to my mother, Nancy Whipple Lord, for teaching me to knit, and to my late grandmother Flora Hall Whipple for teaching her to knit. And heartfelt thanks to my wonderful husband David and my son Alexander for patience and understanding and support! And merci to Tunde Schwartz for always being there!

Stockists

The delicious yarns and products used in this book are available from the following distributors. You can always depend on these labels for yarns that are of the finest quality. Check their websites for shops in your area, or for products available online.

Yarns

Berroco
14 Elmdale Road
PO Box 367
Uxbridge, MA 01569-0367
508-278-2527
www.berroco.com

Manos Del Uruguay
Design Source, US Distributor
PO Box 770
Stoneham, MA 02155
888-566-9970

Rowan Yarns from Westminster Fibers
5 Northern Boulevard
Amherst, NH 03031
603-886-5041
www.knitrowan.com

Brown Sheep
100662 County Road 16
Mitchell, NE 69357
308-635-2198
www.brownsheep.com

The Fibre Company
144 Fore Street
Studio 1-D
Portland, ME 04101
207-761-9992
www.thefibreco.com

Needles

Addi Turbos from Skacel Collection, Inc.
224 SW 12th Street
Renton, WA 98055
213-854-2710

Buttons

Zecca (Fimo buttons)
PO Box 215
North Egremont, MA 01252
413-528-0066
www.zecca.net

Central Yarn
53 Oak Street
Portland, ME 04101
207-775-0852
www.centralyarn.com

Dog Bed Inserts

Fetch
195 Commercial Street
Portland, ME 04101
207.773.5450
www.fetchportland.com

Knitter's Abbreviations

approx	Approximately	**psso**	Pass the slipped stitch over the last stitch worked
beg	Beginning	**rem**	Remaining
CC	Contrasting color	**rep**	Repeat(s)
cont	Continue(ing)s	**rev St st**	Reverse stockinette stitch—k all WS rows, p all RS rows
CN	Cable needle		
Dec (s)	Decrease(s)	**rib**	Rib(bing)
dpn	Double-pointed needle	**rnd(s)**	Round(s) in circular knitting
est	Established	**RS**	Right side
garter	Knit all stitches and/or rows	**SKP**	slip 1, knit 1, pass slipped stitch over
inc (s)	Increase(s)	**sl**	Slip(ed) (ping). Slip stitches from left hand needle to right hand needle
k	Knit		
k2tog	Knit two stitches together	**ssk**	Slip 1, slip 1, knit 1
M1	Make one stitch	**st(s)**	Stitch(es)
MC	Main color	**St st**	Stockinette stitch—k all RS rows, p all WS rows
p	Purl		
p2tog	Purl two stitches together	**tog**	Together
pat (s)	Pattern(s)	**WS**	Wrong side

Needle Conversions

METRIC (MM)	US	OLD UK
2	0	14
2.25	1	13
2.5		
2.75	2	12
3		
3.25	3	10
3.5	4	
3.75		
4	6	8
4.5	7	7
5	8	6
5.5	9	5
6	10	4
6.5	10.5	3
7		2
7.5		1
8	11	0
9	13	00
10	15	000